IMAGES
of America

THE GRAND CANYON
NATIVE PEOPLE AND EARLY VISITORS

Hemis Kachina tributes Home Coming or Harvest. This style of Kachina sculpture was prevalent during the late 1800s and early 1900s. (Sculpture by Ciro Lo Pinto, Hopi; photographed by Jay M. Arancio.)

IMAGES
of America

THE GRAND CANYON

NATIVE PEOPLE AND EARLY VISITORS

Kenneth D. Shields Jr.

ARCADIA
PUBLISHING

Published by Arcadia Publishing
Charleston, South Carolina

Printed in the United States of America

Library of Congress Catalog Card Number: 00107498

For all general information contact Arcadia Publishing at:
Telephone 843-853-2070
Fax 843-853-0044
E-mail sales@arcadiapublishing.com
For customer service and orders:
Toll-Free 1-888-313-2665

Visit us on the Internet at www.arcadiapublishing.com

DEDICATION

In honor and memory of Mr. David Humphrey Scott.

It was David's father, Dudley, who pioneered the Southwest desert in the 1920s and '30s, and took such wonderful photographs of the people and the place. David Humphrey Scott grew up on the grounds of Euclid Beach Park, a lakeside amusement park in Cleveland, Ohio, where his father Dudley was chief engineer.

Thank you, Mr. Scott, for the invitation as well as the strength to do this work. You have the kindest of families. Like me, they cherish your memory and, most of all, your many accomplishments.

CONTENTS

ACKNOWLEDGMENTS

My sincere thanks go to my associate, Linda, a most unique and wonderful lady who provides moral support and emotional insight. It was her loving patience and professional expertise that orchestrated and fostered an author for the people.

I also express my appreciation to Carol Zegarac and the other family members of David Humphrey Scott of Cleveland, Ohio. During the research for this book, it was David and his wife, Georgene, who introduced me to the collection of photographs taken by David's father, Dudley. They and their children took the time to give me the insight needed to fully appreciate the work of Dudley and his wife, Louise.

I would like to thank Colleen L. Hyde, Museum Technician of the National Park Service, for her constant support with this project. Her extensive knowledge of the Grand Canyon National Park's Museum Collection helpfully guided me through the archives. I also thank Colleen for her tireless efforts and gracious service in providing these photographs.

To Mr. David Blacker an acknowledgement is given for his assistance and kind demeanor. In addition, the author acknowledges the Grand Canyon Association for their continued efforts to preserve and protect the park from modern pollutants and over-aggressive visitors. My thanks also go to AmFac Parks and Resorts for their permission to use photographs of the Fred Harvey Company.

I extend special thanks to Jay M. Arancio of Media Works. His valuable time and outstanding digital image dexterity during the scanning and presentation of the photographs proved invaluable. Jay also photographed the Kachina sculptures. Thanks go to Ciro Lo Pinto, a skilled wood carver, who allowed us to present a sample of his Hopi Kachina sculptures and dolls in this text.

I would like to thank Scott L. Zanger for his review and word processing assistance. His editing comments helped make writing the book an enjoyable experience. Thanks, too, to Evan Stampoulos for his contribution to this work.

Special thanks go to my wife, Judy, for her support and encouragement, and to my children Tammy, Toni, Kenny, and Stephanie for their love and understanding.

INTRODUCTION

Today's visitors to the Grand Canyon see little of the formative period in which early visitors met the canyon's original inhabitants. For hundreds of years, natives resided peacefully within the rim, carving out a life of basic survival and spirituality. Needless to say, the appearance of white faces peaked more than curiosity within the resident tribes.

The period between 1890 and 1930 was a time of both excitement and impending conflict. On the one hand, the first appearance of white visitors—in the form of prospectors, ranchers, photographers, and wealthy travelers—allowed the subsequent opening of the Grand Canyon to generations of enthralled tourists. On the other hand, it was the unchecked fascination of these early visitors that would contribute to the demise of the very people and landscape they had come to admire.

This book aims to portray, through these extraordinary vintage images, the formative period of the modern history of the Grand Canyon. The photographs have been selected from a number of sources, but the one of particular interest is the Dudley Scott Collection. This collection consists of photographs taken by one of the first and most famous visitors, many of which have never been seen in print.

Through working with these extraordinary images, the author realized that the traditional approach to history, that of bringing the story forward, would not work in this case. The story had to be told in reverse. Readers would look backward through the eyes of today's descendants to find traces and discover clues of the ancient Pueblo people, the miners, prospectors, cowboys, and visitors.

What can be told are attempts of portraying a life and culture as evidenced by pieces of pottery, broken sandstone walls, and images painted in long-abandoned caves. The objective account, no matter how scientifically accurate, would fail to reveal that which is indeed most central—the spirit of a people who have survived for centuries.

This book that you now hold in your hands is representative of a tiny fragment of time stretching back over 75 years from the present, yet which manages to uniquely capture a real sense of spirit. Utilizing the images on these pages as "eyes" to the past, the reader can begin to "feel" an understanding of the rich legacy that is truly a natural resource for all of us to appreciate.

According to the National Park Service, there are currently at least five different Indian groups in the area of the Grand Canyon, each with its own language, customs, and beliefs. The Havasupai, the People of the Blue Green Water, still occupy their traditional lands in Cataract Canyon. The Hualapai maintain an area on the south rim. To the east, the park is bordered by the Navajo Nation. The Paiute live around Pipe Springs on the Arizona side to the north. The Zuni Nation of New Mexico trace a heritage to Ribbon Falls within the Canyon. The Pueblo Indians settled in the southwestern part of the United States. Their villages were found in areas of five different states: Arizona, Nevada, New Mexico, Utah, and Colorado.

A common denominator for most of them is their connection to a prehistoric people often referred to as the Anasazi, a Navajo word meaning "ancient ones," or Hitsatsinom, a Hopi word which references their ancestors. In writing the text for this book, the author has recognized some of the sensitive subject matter involved, and has made every effort to avoid "European" labels which might be offensive to any particular tribe.

The pages which follow are an attempt to bring life to this place. The canyon is not now, nor ever was, as silent, unmoving, and still as it appears from its rim. It is to help with this life-giving process that, by putting people in this place, we begin to see another dimension emerge, thus providing the human layers—so often overlooked—which nonetheless coated the canyon walls with a kind of human pallet of color and culture all their own.

Our pictorial journey takes us on a clearly circular route. Early visitors had visions of wealth and riches. They would dig in these walls and mine whatever of value was held within. Yet the very grandeur of the canyon outweighed its exploitation, and mining gave way to tourism. While surely more passive an enterprise, tourism was not without its difficulties. Tourists were not always as "passive" as one would think. Soon it was not enough to simply stand at the edges and contemplate, one would travel down within it, along the narrow paths or braving the twists and turns of the Colorado River. Without careful monitoring and vigilance, tourists can damage even the most beautiful and pristine of places. Other tourists took to the air. Enterprising pilots would offer flights into the canyon, the drone of their piston-driven engines piercing the silence. Today there is a determined effort on the part of those dedicated rangers of the Grand Canyon National Park Service to preserve and protect this national treasure so that, for countless generations to come, old and young alike may find inspiration here.

The author's approach is meant to be as light and breezy as the gentle winds that float up the sheer walls from the canyon floor below, welcoming each new visitor to the rim as if he were the very first.

Author, Kenneth D. Shields Jr.: Grass Dancer. (for more Arcadia books by Mr. Shields, visit *www.Tribe–Net.com.*)

One

THE BASKETMAKERS

There is a place in the American Southwest, near the area of the Grand Canyon, that was the home of a group of people that scientists call the Anasazi, a Navajo Indian word. About 2,000 years ago, these Pueblo people learned to survive in extremely harsh conditions and for more than 1,000 years thrived there. Then, they simply disappeared.

They were called the Basketmakers, because they wove beautiful baskets and sandals from the bark of trees and plant fibers. Pictured here is a Havasupai woman, Jeck-spa-na-pi's wife, making one of these baskets. It took great patience and skill to construct such items. Indian people love round things as they believe the Great Spirit also loves round things, such as the earth and its seasons. In making circular objects these Basketmakers were creating tokens of remembrance and respect. (Grand Canyon National Park #10097; c. 1898.)

For eons the land has pre-existed man. Though the terrain is harsh and dangerous, early man survived. These are badlands, a place worth discovering. Through adaptation and help from some unknown power, this land of desolation became home. This photo was taken at Moran Point in Grand Canyon National Park, Arizona. (GCNP #8243; *c.* 1940.)

The area of the Pueblo people is the high plateau country of northern Arizona, the southern edge of Utah, southwestern Colorado, and most of northern New Mexico. Parts are deserts, parts are covered with coniferous forests, and the terrain is cut with deep river arroyos and canyons. (GCNP #6819. Photo Courtesy of Dudley Scott Collection; *c.* 1925.)

The climate in the Southwest is dry, and temperatures can vary from extremely hot to quite cold. There is a demonstrated cultural continuity present in Pueblo Indian descendent culture. (GCNP Museum. Dudley Scott Collection; *c.* 1925.)

Traces of these peaceful people dot the landscape of the great Southwest. They are reminders of a once proud and noble people. Scientists offer varied theories as to why these people disappeared—including drought, disease, and invasion by neighboring tribes. The Indians have their own ideas and beliefs as to what happened. (GCNP Museum. Dudley Scott Collection; *c.* 1925.)

Ruins of thousands of these Anasazi buildings still stand. This ancient foyer was built with mathematical precision. The word "Anasazi" is a collective reference to prehistoric Pueblo people who lived in the Southwest centuries ago. Although the term is a Navajo word meaning "Ancient Ones," and became standard usage in the 1930s, the reference is offensive to other tribes in the region. (GCNP Museum. Dudley Scott Collection; *c.* 1925.)

Originally, the Basketmakers were nomadic hunters and gatherers. The men and boys used nets for catching rabbits and spears for hunting larger animals such as deer, bison, and wild sheep. Women and girls gathered roots, cactus, flowers, pine nuts, and plants. In this photo we see a Havasupai girl coating one of her baskets with pitch. This natural epoxy was found in trees. This made for a waterproof container. The girl clearly shows her enjoyment at what she is doing. Having the ability to transport water in baskets gave people such as the Havasupai the ability to move around more freely. (GCNP #10096; c. 1898.)

The cultural heritage of today's Pueblo Indian is easily demonstrated in the areas where present Indians still live on sites and in towns of their ancestors. These women are from the Nu-A-Gun-Tits tribe of the Colorado Valley. Hats worn by these people are very similar to those worn by the Tlingit tribe located on the northwest coast. Many similarities exist among the tribes throughout the continent. These women were photographed in the Colorado Valley during Major Powell's ethnographic expedition in 1873, during which he charted the turbulent waters of the Colorado River. (GCNP #8967; c. 1873.)

White explorers were fascinated with early Native American architecture. Dwellings were cool in summer and warm in winter. The top floor could be a granary. Note the poles for supporting struts and for aerial "walkways." (GCNP Museum. Dudley Scott Collection; c. 1925.)

Ruins of the ancient peoples were discovered by the whites. Scholars, photographers, and others saw this as an opportunity to explore early civilization. Such photos are now in archives and personal collections. Here, a couple begins their own early exploration. (GCNP Museum. Dudley Scott Collection; c. 1925.)

When the white man came and discovered pictographs, they gave evidence of some kind of civilization. Through the process of searching and inquiring, the land unveiled its secrets. Concealed amid rocks and crevices, they found a civilization which had long passed on. (GCNP Museum. Dudley Scott Collection; c. 1925.)

The Pueblo Indians traded their pottery and baskets with numerous people of Mexico for copper bells, shells, and other decorative items.

For the people of the Grand Canyon, the loom was an instrument of great worth. Primitive by modern standards, it was years ahead in technology during the period of the ancients. Some women often wove turkey feathers into their blankets in order to make them warmer. (GCNP #6773. Dudley Scott Collection; c. 1925.)

From a distance, the white man determined strategic locations from which these ancients sought to live out their lives. From here, the dwellings appear to be a place of refuge. Enemies in those days were numerous. Altercations over food and hunting grounds may be one explanation. (GCNP Museum. Dudley Scott Collection; c. 1925)

More than 700 years ago (200 years before the first Europeans came to America), the Anasazi disappeared from the American Southwest. Built into solid rock, homes were fashioned with huge hewn stone blocks, a technology little known today. Overhangs were for protection from above. Pathways were well hidden and afforded good transportation in and out of this quiet village. (GCNP Museum. Dudley Scott Collection; c. 1925.)

The Eastern Court of Araibi is pictured above. Homes were no longer built into solid walls. Instead, they became communities where hundreds (rather than mere small families) could congregate. Trading and bartering soon followed. (GCNP #12075; c. 1873.)

Spanish explorers came to this area in the 1600s. They hoped to find gold and minerals in the canyon walls. (Photo from author's private collection.)

The discovery of the bow and arrow had the effect of increasing the food supply. The arrow, compared to the spear, enabled the hunter to kill from a greater distance and have far greater accuracy. Women often were hunters also and took their children with them. While hunting, the women gathered a special kind of reed and straw for weaving. Here, a baby enjoys the ride. (GCNP #5117; c. 1898.)

Looking over the vast canyon, it seems impossible that this area could sustain life. Yet, for centuries it has been the home of many Indian groups. (Photo from author's private collection.)

Here, a short-haired Havasupai woman is carrying a Kathak burden basket. It was the custom for women not to show their faces. Beautiful hand-made shawls and baskets reveal a most colorful character. Women wove baskets and sandals from tree bark and yucca fibers. (GCNP #829; 1902 photo by Henry Peabody.)

A Havasupai couple sits here on the ground. The woman pictured is holding an empty cradle board. These people adored children and held them in high esteem. To make a cradle board was a tribute to the child. The Pueblo mothers carried their babies on their backs, strapped to a cradle board. (GCNP #10095; c. 1898.)

Among all Anasazi structures, kivas are the most interesting for archaeologists. Unlike the square, above-ground dwellings, kivas were usually round, partially subterranean, and entered only through a hole in the roof. As ceremonial structures, kivas follow a cultural line extending to the Hopi descendants of today. A fireplace stood at the center of the floor, and smoke escaped through a hole in the roof. Another small hole in the floor called the "sipaipu," or spirit hole, was believed to be the opening through which the first people, the people from the underground (the Third World), entered this, the Fourth World. (GCNP. Dudley Scott Collection; c. 1925.)

Two

FOOTPRINTS OVER THE FOURTH WORLD

The oral tradition of the Hopi explains that the Pueblo people had a covenant with the spirit that guarded them. This was a promise to give them stewardship of their land if they migrated and to place their "footprints over the Fourth World" in the form of pictographs and shrines. Seen here is a pictograph panel on Point Sublime Cliff on the North Rim of the Grand Canyon. Whoever did this must have been agile and had some technical knowledge of climbing. (GCNP #5743; c. 1931.)

These prehistoric petroglyphs painted on a roof of a cave could only be symbolic of intelligent life. Could it be man? Might it be some ancient astral visitor? The variety of cryptic designs allows the observer a wondering mind. (GCNP #7157; c. 1930.)

During the mid-thirteenth century, the Hopis moved to three flat-topped hills called mesas. They are the northern prongs of the Black Mesa of Arizona. From east to west, the hills were given names: First Mesa, Second Mesa, and Third Mesa. Each mesa can be seen from the other. This photo, taken in 1918, is a street scene of Mishongnova, Hopi, Second Mesa. (GCNP #11326.)

This is very cryptographic artwork. Deer, rabbits, ducks, roadrunners, bears, rattlesnakes, and other sacred symbols revolve around a mythical bird. Northern tribes of the United States regard this winged entity as the "Thunderbird." A sacred being living in the sky, the Thunderbird is seen amid the harmony and movement of the natural surroundings. (GCNP Museum. Dudley Scott Collection; *c.* 1925.)

These youngsters appear to be waiting for a school bus. Although schools were available, sometimes they were far away. Willing to learn, the children caught onto studies quickly and shared what knowledge they had with others. (GCNP Museum. Dudley Scott Collection; *c.* 1925.)

When the river flowed at its normal rate, crops were planted, and the soil was rich and moist. But too often, droughts occurred, and the rivers became small streams slowing crop growth and lowering grazing land for herds. (Photo from author's private collection).

Built on "terraces," the Pueblo village appears as a modern-day apartment complex. Note the round, stone oven in the center of the photo. Cornmeal was baked into a kind of bread, or mixed with meat, beans, and other kinds of food to make soups and stews. (GCNP Museum. Dudley Scott Collection; c. 1925.)

The Pueblo people led hard lives. The cliffs on which many of their pueblos were perched are high and steep. Hauling stones for cutting had to be a tedious task involving much hard work. With entire families united together in accomplishing the chore, the work became bearable. As is evident, mathematics played an important role in ancient architecture. (Dudley Scott Collection; c. 1925.)

Havasupai girls play a game of "Hui-ta-qui-chi-ka." Dressed in Anglo clothes, they demonstrate an ancient game. Anglo influence was fast becoming widespread. (GCNP #10094; c. 1898.)

Father and son are on an outing. Teaching children about life prepared them for living their own lives. To have a son was to have future posterity to lead the tribe. (GCNP Museum. Dudley Scott Collection; *c.* 1925.)

7514. Hopi House, Grand Canyon, Arizona

This pre-1920s postcard shows the Hopi House, Grand Canyon, Arizona, which copied the Hopi Mesa architecture. (GCNP #8233B.)

Native artisans are pictured on Hopi House roof, Grand Canyon, Arizona. Weaving and making pottery was an art. Hairstyling was practiced to improve womanly beauty and for ceremonials. When girls were old enough for marriage, their hair was fashioned into a squash blossom. The hair was parted in the middle, and each side was wound in a figure-eight around a bent willow form. (GCNP #9856A.)

Taking an early stroll, this inhabitant of the village may be going out to inspect livestock. Note the makeshift "shades" in the village foreground. (GCNP Museum. Dudley Scott Collection; *c.* 1925.)

Pueblo farming was difficult because of the frequent droughts, high winds, and shifting sands common to the region. Water was scarce, and ditches were dug to irrigate planting areas. They planted near large streams, which allowed them to benefit from the overflow of a sudden cloudburst. (GCNP Museum. Dudley Scott Collection; *c.* 1925.)

While mother is weaving, a boy plays outside. Climbing is always in a child's curriculum. Since trees are sparse, this ladder will have to do. (GCNP Museum. Dudley Scott Collection; *c.* 1925.)

Shown above is a street scene. Like modern day metropolises, Native Americans enjoyed city life. Burros afforded slow transportation, but they were reliable, and children had them as pets. (GCNP #11327.)

This view shows a Supai woman with a white burro, and a man who might be C. Osborn of Flagstaff. Some of these valleys contained balanced rocks, like those shown here. Nature has its own way of doing things. These people may have been travelling to do some trading. (GCNP #8397; November 16, 1895.)

An ancient people, the Havasupai call this "Guardians of the Havasupai, Corn Rocks," or "Wick-A-Leva." So, after all, there was intelligent life living in these harsh lands. Very spiritual, the Havasupai understood nature and its importance to man. These towering behemoths withstood centuries of erosion, fortifying the assumption of the ancients that nature was created before man, and therefore has stronger natural powers. (National Park Service. Grand Canyon National Park, #229; May 5, 1944.)

From ancient knowledge of housing, these inhabitants built the first condominium-type dwellings. In case of emergency, ladders could be pulled up and kept inside, affording safety for the people. (GCNP #12074; January 21, 1918.)

Three

MOTHER EARTH'S GIFTS

Pueblo people believed that Mother Earth would provide everything they needed to sustain life. The animals portrayed on their pottery were lively, showing they were given bountiful supply of wild game such as deer, elk, mountain sheep, rabbits, squirrels, and water fowl. During the Wheeler Expedition it was discovered that the ancient inhabitants were not always warriors and hunters. This photo credits them with being arts and crafts people. (GCNP #9903; c. 1873.)

As Indian customs waned, white influence became more prevalent. Here Chief Watahomigie holds a scythe. The Indians never had this metal instrument, but constructed them of bone or rock. Pausing, he rests while working in an alfalfa field. The Havasupai Indians traditionally had two chiefs: the so-called "War Chief" who handled defense matters, and another who dealt with more peaceful duties. (GCNP #232; c. 1944.)

Corn was the most important crop. The Pueblos did not plow; they would leave the crusty cover of the earth untouched to protect the dampness underneath. Corn was also important to their religious beliefs. The creation story of several of these Indian groups involved corn plants. Many important ceremonial rituals centered around the planting and harvesting of the corn. (Dudley Scott Collection; c. 1926.)

A cliff ruin, hidden for centuries, is pictured in Nankowap. Entrance to the dwelling proved difficult. The ancients who lived here at one time have disappeared. We see visible signs of that fact. What stories they could have told! These occupants built their homes to withstand eons of time. (GCNP #5984; c. 1935.)

An attractive young lady inspects a stone oven. In these ovens, cornmeal was baked into bread. The cornmeal was gritty because grains of rock from the sandstone metate and mano rubbed off in the grinding process. This gritty cornmeal, a main part of their diet, probably accounted for the bad teeth of many of the Pueblo Indians. Behind her is a metal wagon, evidence of playful children nearby. Ladders afforded access to the above "flats." (GCNP Museum. Dudley Scott Collection; c. 1925.)

This photograph shows a street scene in Walpi Village on Hopi First Mesa. The key to living in the desert is water. All life in the Pueblo depended upon a close and constant supply, as it was needed to make pottery, grow crops, water the sheep, and even to make adobe for houses. (GCNP #11328; c. 1918.)

During the mother's breaks between work, children play. This one is about to sneeze. The sun's rays bring this on when a child awakens from a daily nap. This little girl is dressed in light clothing to ward off the heat. Note the tattered stockings similar to "puttees" worn by soldiers. (GCNP Museum. Dudley Scott Collection; *c.* 1925.)

Here is a view down and over the cobble wall at the village of Moenkopi. Note the cornfields behind. (GCNP #6806. Dudley Scott Collection; *c.* 1926.)

A Havasupai Indian girl is pictured here. This could be witness of a "purification" ceremony, a ritual preparing a young girl for womanhood. Note the very intricate shawl which brings much dazzle to the beautiful girl. (GCNP #822. Photo by Henry G. Peabody; *c.* 1902.)

Since the 1600s, sheep have been a valuable part of Navajo life. To own a flock was a symbol of a family's well being. Everyone joined in to help raise them. The sheep knew their owner's voice and came whenever called. (GCNP #6772. Dudley Scott Collection; *c.* 1925.)

A young male Havasupai Indian with long hair stands next to a saddled pony. Indians were avid and accomplished horsemen. Horses were revered, and to have one conferred status. Wiry and agile, this young warrior reveals a man to be reckoned with. (GCNP #827. Photo by Henry G. Peabody; *c.* 1902.)

The Indian people built structures with what they could find. Imagination and ingenuity were always foremost in their minds. At left is a sheep corral and an area for counting them. (GCNP, Dudley Scott Collection; c. 1925.)

This is a weaver's loom. An intricate device, it was ingeniously made. Before sheep's wool could be woven on a loom, it was "carded" to make it free from knots. It was then dyed using natural sources, spun, and readied to be woven. Today, Navajo women still weave colorful belts, rugs, and blankets from homespun wool. Some still use natural vegetable dyes to create colors that their grandmothers used. (GCNP #6774; c. 1925.)

As there were no schools, boys were taught practical skills from their fathers. Tending flocks of sheep and goats required good roping techniques. In this photo, a Navajo boy practices his roping talents on a badger from horseback. (GCNP #6779A. Dudley Scott Collection; c. 1926.)

Pictured is a pack string southwest of Mount Sinyella during the Little Horse Expedition. These animals were sought after because of their rarity. The little horses were also wild. (GCNP #7142.)

Havasupai guides J. Jones and Claude Watohomige are shown in camp as part of the Little Horse Expedition. Working long hours, these men reveal their toughness by living in this forbidden wilderness. (GCNP #7152; *c.* 1938.)

Navajo families made their homes, called hogans, of wooden poles, tree bark, and mud. The homes were built with support poles. The doorway of each hogan opened to the east so Navajos could welcome the morning sun. To awaken and rise with the sun was important to a healthy life. (GCNP #6771. Dudley Scott Collection; c. 1925.)

This Havasupai Indian girl in long dress stands facing the camera and holding a woven basket. Although water was sometimes scarce, the people kept good personal hygiene. From a diet of fresh vegetables and little meat, these people retained youthful good looks. Note their shiny, healthy, black hair—evidence of a wholesome diet. (GCNP #831. Photo by Henry G. Peabody; *c.* 1902.)

Hopi religion cannot be separated from everyday life. The rituals performed represent the people's role as caretakers of the earth. Their pueblos provided outdoor plazas where they could gather to play music and sing and dance. (GCNP #5419. Photo by the Fred Harvey Company; *c.* 1933.)

A patriarch sits outside resting. Here, Havasupai Chief Kohot sits on a blanket in front of his house. (GCNP #10091; *c.* 1898.)

Two men with a mountain lion skin are shown at the range operations building. Hunting could also be a bounty. Sheepherders sometimes had their animals ravaged by wild animals. By calling in local people, they tracked and brought the offending animal in. (GCNP #133; c. 1931.)

Four

EARTH, WIND, AND WATER

The early Pueblo Indians had a close relationship with every living thing. Life and spirit lived in the mountains, the rivers, and the sky. Three vital forces—earth, wind, and water—were a part of every Indian's daily life. These forces were interdependent and respected. They believed that there is good within all things, but that evil and danger can result when the normal balance of the universe is disturbed.

In this photo, an elderly Havasupai gentleman walks with his cane. It was believed in ancient custom that when a man had three legs, his life was nearly at its end. It meant that with old age came walking with a cane as support for tired legs, from walking long years on the earth. This man had farm animals and grew corn. (GCNP #10093; c. 1898.)

"There's a new sheriff in town!" Posing beside his automobile, an unidentified gentleman pauses in front of an adobe structure. As the glass windows suggest, this one is of a more modern type. (GCNP Museum. Dudley Scott Collection; *c.* 1925.)

Mr. and Mrs. Dudley Scott's automobile is shown carefully climbing one of the many steep canyon walls. (GCNP Museum. Dudley Scott Collection; *c.* 1929.)

Living in the community, a man could do as he pleased. This man is standing outside his property. Note the white influence in terms of the trousers, belt, shoes, and shirt. (GCNP Museum. Dudley Scott Collection; *c.* 1925.)

This pueblo structure manifests a more modern look. Sandstone blocks are stacked like bricks and cemented with adobe. When the adobe dried, it was hard and waterproof. (GCNP Museum. Dudley Scott Collection; *c.* 1925.)

Trading posts were not uncommon. Mail comes in once a week, and goods are usually in small supply. Here a visitor enjoys the tranquility found in the Grand Canyon area. Gasoline was rather scarce, and travelers had to make plans carefully in order that they not prematurely run out. (GCNP Museum. Dudley Scott Collection; *c.* 1925.)

The road seems to stretch out for miles and miles. (GCNP Museum. Dudley Scott Collection; *c.* 1925.)

Adhering to traditional ways, some families still have living arrangements together. In here could be as many as five to ten families. Again note the round, stone ovens. (GCNP Museum. Dudley Scott Collection; *c.* 1925.)

Observing a young mother at her labor is quite satisfying. Learning to weave at a tender age, she will turn an empty loom into a beautiful piece of art. (GCNP Museum. Dudley Scott Collection; *c.* 1925.)

When they weren't busy doing homemaking chores, women did other things. Equestrian ability was not limited to men. Women also enjoyed it. Keeping a firm rein gave the horse a noble look. This one has a saddle probably acquired through bartering with white horsemen. (GCNP Museum. Dudley Scott Collection; c. 1925.)

This is a fine example of a small city. The lady poses by a sign that could read "Welcome." Note the round turtle-like structures in the left foreground. Huge loaves of homemade bread were baked in these stone ovens. (GCNP Museum. Dudley Scott Collection; c. 1925.)

This photo is labeled "Nina Grey Hair's Camp. Party stranded south of Park. Cared for by rangers." Misfortune was not an uncommon experience. Because of low rainfall, food became scarce. Although a hardy people, they still must have provisions. (GCNP #166; *c.* 1930.)

Here is a small "spread" in the Hopi village of Moenkopi. Like the white homesteaders, the Indian people made use of animals for a living. As evidenced here, a rancher is making a living on his own. (GCNP #6802. Dudley Scott Collection; *c.* 1925.)

This view shows a Zuni village with corn and ovens. Generations later, posterity took charge. Building dwellings on the flats became the norm. (GCNP #11339; *c.* 1918.)

Chief Manakadja poses with a young child outside a dirt-roof house. (GCNP #190; *c.* 1938.)

This Havasupai, "Cick-a-pan-a-gi," is holding a rifle. His saddle horse in the background, this Indian favors the famed Winchester Model 1873 lever action rifle. Small ponies were hardy little horses and could thrive on very little. (GCNP #10090; *c.* 1898.)

Two Supai men are shown with their mounts, and a woman stands outside. Cabins such as this one were placed as rest areas. Being miles from civilization, it was good to have such lodges. (GCNP #189; c. 1938.)

Although small cities thrived, there were still those attached to the "old way." Living outside the "city limits," they took up residence. Here, a 107-year-old Havasupai woman suns herself. Happy with the way things are, she holds onto traditional housing. (GCNP #1214; c. 1938.)

Much of a woman's time was spent grinding corn and cooking. The corn was ground in a mill made of a coarse rock, usually sandstone. Kernels of corn were placed on a slab and rubbed against it by means of a rounded rock. In this photo, a white-haired Havasupai woman is grinding her corn. Baskets and tin cans surround her. Corn was the staff of life for these people. From that, the "Corn Dance" came into notoriety with different tribes. (GCNP #10092; *c.* 1900.)

Five

PUEBLO LIFE

The Pueblo Indians of the Southwest survived the intrusion first of the Spaniards in search of gold, and later the Anglo settlers in search of land, riches, and adventure. In time, these peaceful people became the most populous of American Indian tribes.

Seated outside his house, this man enjoys the shade. Note the metal cooking pots hanging on the outer wall. (GCNP Museum. Dudley Scott Collection; c. 1925.)

From a distance, this adobe structure could be home to a wealthy individual. Note the glass doors and windows as well as the stone enclosure. (GCNP Museum. Dudley Scott Collection; c. 1925.)

A citizen is about to enter a structure that could be an early business. Note the screen door and sign on the outside wall. Women dressed in shawls to protect them from the searing sun. (GCNP Museum. Dudley Scott Collection; c. 1925.)

These two men, like many Hopi, prefer to stay in their mesa homes and farm as their ancestors did for centuries before them. (GCNP #5416A; *c.* 1933.)

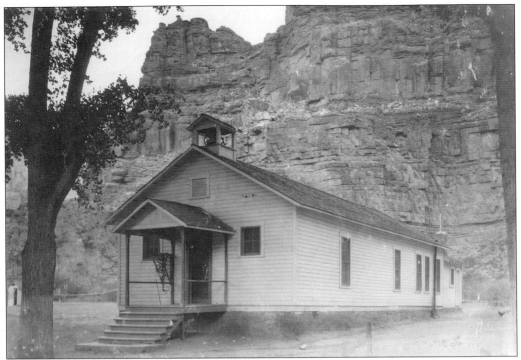

This is a school house at Havasupai. Indian children looked forward to learning, and once given the opportunity to be educated, learned quickly. Returning home, they were excited about what knowledge they had received. Sometimes they taught their parents, because they did not know how to read or write. (GCNP #179; *c.* 1938.)

These Supai boys are playing school games. Teamwork was the norm for Native Americans. During this time, English was being introduced as a second language. A time of bilingual education was now in the making. To live two cultures would have its advantages in future years. (GCNP #180; *c.* 1938.)

As white influence spread, so did medical assistance. Susceptible to disease, the Indians of this region suffered many deaths because they were not immune. Smallpox and diphtheria were horrendous. Here is a nurse's residence in a Supai village where the people came to receive inoculations. (GCNP #186; c. 1938.)

Indians did far more than farm the land. Here a congregation of tribal members meet together in council in 1947. Officials from the government looked in on them frequently. They stand together, men from the new world and men from the old. This particular photo was taken on the occasion of a meeting of the entire Havasupai Tribal Council at Grand Canyon Village on September 12, 1947. (GCNP #982.)

Navajo children are shown gathered by a "Trading Post" water tank. (GCNP #6784. Dudley Scott Collection; *c.* 1926.)

From Athabascan stock, the Navajo are famous for their weaving, horse breeding, and rearing of sheep and goats. As always, a child is nearby to render assistance when needed. (GCNP #6776. Dudley Scott Collection; *c.* 1925.)

Changes had indeed occurred. From living among the rocks in nearby mountains, people now moved to lower areas. Building fences and raising sheep and cattle, they were becoming prosperous. (GCNP Museum. Dudley Scott Collection; *c.* 1925.)

Here, Pete Mongola's Supai wife kneels on a blanket. Shelters were fashioned in different ways, and women had dominion over the house. (GCNP #183; *c.* 1938.)

This place of worship shows how Catholic influence abounded among desert tribes. A peaceful people, they readily accepted gospel teachings and remained obedient to them. This is a beautiful structure situated in a low valley. Note the cross on top of the gate. (Dudley Scott Collection; *c.* 1926.)

This Hopi residence in Menkoi shows a relationship to the neighborhood building. (GCNP #6805. Dudley Scott Collection; *c.* 1926.)

Storm Over First Mesa. Portrayed in this Kachina sculpture is "Nuvak'chin Mana," or the Snow Maiden. She is shown protecting the mesa.

The Kachina beliefs can be traced to the social and religious life of the Puebloans. Today's Kachinas are believed to be messengers between the people and the forces that control the universe. The Kachinas will bring rain to the dry desert so that crops will grow. Each Kachina has a name, a distinctive costume, and a face represented by a sacred mask. (Sculpture by Ciro Lo Pinto, Hopi; photographed by Jay M. Arancio.)

This is a look down "Main Street." Imagine, if you will, hundreds of livestock herded through here to grazing and watering areas. Today, communities such as this still thrive in the southwest. (GCNP Museum. Dudley Scott Collection; *c.* 1925.)

Lowland communities housed families. Here, visitors take advantage by posing for a photograph. The automobile was a sight to see for the Native Americans. Streams were used for drinking, bathing, laundering, and watering the animals. Drinking was done upstream. (GCNP Museum. Dudley Scott Collection; *c.* 1925.)

The dry plateau regions today are different from the tree-lined floodplains of 225 million years ago, during what is called the Triassic Period. Many traces of this geologic period remain in the form of petrified wood or other fossils. A large collection, such as these petrified logs, are found in the Petrified Forest National Park in Arizona.

In the mid-1800s, U.S. Army mappers and surveyors came to this area and carried back east stories of the remarkable Painted Desert and petrified wood. Next, farmers, ranchers, and sightseers made their way into the area to see for themselves. In 1906, related "forests" were set aside as protected areas. (Photo from author's private collection.)

Pictured is a Navajo horseman wearing a large hat, seated on his mount. Note the bundle of gear tied behind the saddle. The outdoors was second nature to "Indian cowboys." (GCNP #6650; c. 1930.)

With a wondering air about her, a lady surveys an ancient culture on this "Main Street." Rain is scarce, as portrayed by clouds too high to afford much needed moisture. Usually the huge "thunderhead" clouds are those that predict rain. (GCNP Museum. Dudley Scott Collection; c. 1925.)

While all the schooling children were learning about the modern world, the elderly still adhered to ancient ways and customs. Preparing a sacred sand painting, these men will teach children ways to enhance the inner spirit. Both ways of teaching imparted important, though different, principles. This particular sand painting was being prepared for the dedication of "El Navajo Hotel" in Gallup, New Mexico, on May 26, 1923. (GCNP #15247.)

Droughts and floods made farming and grazing more and more difficult. The people would turn to their religion and Kachinas to help them through the hard times. (Photo from author's private collection.)

Salako Taka is the Hopi Cloud Kachina. The shape of this sculpture resembles a seed pod. (Sculpture by Ciro Lo Pinto, Hopi; photographed by Jay M. Arancio.)

Hototo is the Bear Kachina. Kachina dolls are used to teach children about the spirits that help them. Actual masks and costumes worn during Hopi ceremonies are sacred objects. (Sculpture by Ciro Lo Pinto, Hopi; photographed by Jay M. Arancio.)

The Grand Canyon walls are painted with the history and the culture of Pueblo people. They occupied the area for centuries and learned to use what resources were available to them. Today's society can benefit from the lessons preserved from the past. (Photo from author's private collection.)

To continue the journey of a hidden people, we see them sing a song of victory. Through turbulent years, these tribes prevailed and prospered even during the most grievous of times. Being humble, they thrive today to manifest their destiny, in that they are indeed a chosen people. Singing is sacred to them, and the drum is the heartbeat of generations past. Be still, and you may feel it throb in your own chest. Listen and you will hear the wind whisper their song. (GCNP #12086; *c.* 1905.)

Six

THE SEEKERS

Joe, the burro belonging to prospector Bill Bass, is fully loaded and climbing switchback (meaning zig-zag) on the Topocoba Trail. Similar to the gold rush going on in California, prospectors came to the Grand Canyon in search of riches. Note the difficult canyon terrain.

However, not everyone searched for treasure. Some wanted to capture the canyon's vistas on film. Photographers like Emery and Ellsworth Kolb, and Henry G. Peabody visited the Grand Canyon at the turn of the century. They often rode burros into the canyon, similar to Joe, heavily laden with photographic equipment. (GCNP #828; photo taken by Henry G. Peabody, 1902.)

A hunting party of Native Americans and white trappers take aim with their rifles near Hance Trail. Note Coronado Butte in the distance. (GRCA #8400; November 16, 1895.)

Buffalo Bill Cody and party are christening McKinnon Point on Hance Trail by sinking ship. Many hunters and trappers looked for ways to make themselves rich.(GRCA #5305; November 1892.)

Miners, like Bill Blass, often took their dogs along for companionship. In the late 1800s, the U.S. government promoted the West as a land of abundant resources such as copper, zinc, and lead. (GRCA #833; photo by Henry G. Peabody, *c.* 1899.)

An expedition into the Canyon of Little Horses was undertaken in January of 1938. Here, the party repacks their gear in the rain, following their ascent from Havasu Canyon. (GRCA #7140; January 22, 1938.)

Seth Benjamin Tanner was a prospector and a horse dealer in the canyon area. Tanner Trail bears his name. (GRCA #7060A; *c.* 1885.)

Park Naturalist Edwin McKee measures a horse captured in the Canyon of Little Horses in January 1938. The National Park Service carefully watches the balance of wildlife in the area. (GRCA #5751.)

On the canyon floor, local Indians raise cattle and sheep. Pictured here is a local Navajo tending his herd of cattle. (Courtesy of Dudley Humphrey Scott Collection; c. 1925.)

W.W. Bass and his party camp are pictured at Havasupai Point. Bass is at right with his dog Shep, and George W. James is to Bass's right. (GRCA #824. Photo by Henry G. Peabody; September 1899.)

Scattered throughout the canyon floor were numerous trading posts from which prospectors and miners could obtain supplies. It was the promise of becoming rich that encouraged many to stay. (Courtesy of Dudley Humphrey Scott Collection; c. 1920s.)

Prospectors often sought shelter in these small, galvanized tin shacks. This particular shelter homestead was named "Soap Creek Homestead." (GRCA #14599; *c.* 1927.)

Artie, Slim, and a friend are pictured at camp. Many miners hunted game in the canyon area to supplement their provisions. (Courtesy of the Edward Aschoff Collection; *c.* 1920s.)

South of Phantom Ranch, this mule shelter and stone corral were frequent stopping places for early prospectors. (GRCA #895; *c.* 1930s.)

Cowboys and miners camped close to their claims. Considerable time was consumed recording maps of their various digs. (Courtesy of the Dudley Humphrey Scott Collection; *c.* 1920s.)

Seated in his saddle astride his faithful steed, Fish, cowboy Bill Voight strikes the pose of a lone sentinel. Ranchers and settlers who call this part of the country home face a dry climate and rough terrain. (Courtesy of the Dudley Humphrey Scott Collection; *c.* 1920s.)

The Last Chance Mine and building (lower left) were located at Horseshoe Mesa. Extraction and transportation of ore from the canyon's steep interior to the rim proved a difficult, if not Herculean task. As a result, many mines were soon abandoned. This glass plate photo was taken by Henry G. Peabody in 1899. (GRCA #802.)

Mining and prospecting was not easy, although it was certainly adventurous. Here, prospector Bert Loper sleeps in his camp following a hard day's work along the river. Loper was well-known in these parts as much for his storytelling as for his prospecting. (GRCA #5537; c. 1912.)

In what may appear to some as a grizzly, if not offensive, sight, these two trappers sit proudly on their cabin porch, their feet resting on sets of antlers, displaying some of the furs taken during the winter of 1931 in the canyon and on the north rim. (GRCA #130.)

Seven

THE CHALLENGE
OF THE RIVER

Those who first sought to explore the canyon soon came to the recognition that their journey would not only include the challenge of sheer cliffs and rugged terrain, but an untamed river as well. The mighty Colorado, part of one of the most dominant river systems in the entire southwest, wends its way some 300 miles through the Grand Canyon. The task of traveling the river, or "running" it, has always been and still remains an exciting, and at times, very forbidding challenge. Pictured here is Mr. C.H. Moon, Lees Ferryman, guiding a boat across a handmade landing. (GRCA #6749, Courtesy of the Dudley Humphrey Scott Collection; *c*. 1920s.)

An expedition can run into difficulty in a matter of mere moments. Here members of an early 1891 party of explorers are trying to recover a lost boat in Cataract Canyon. (GRCA #6936.)

This photo, dated 1908, shows park visitors having dismounted their mules and taking a few precious minutes to relax and catch their breath by the edge of the Colorado. (GRCA #4897.)

This flat-bottomed scow at Lee's Ferry carried both cars and wagons across the Colorado River. For years this site served as the only crossing for hundreds of miles up as well as downstream. (Courtesy of the Dudley Humphrey Scott Collection.)

A covered wagon with livestock and two men cross the Colorado River on a barge at Lee's Ferry. (GRCA #14711; *c.* 1900.)

The Deputy Sheriff of Coconino County takes a moment to pose for this picture at Lee's Ferry. (GRCA #6757; Courtesy of the Dudley Humphrey Scott Collection.)

A respite from the hot sun, the Scott's automobile rests in the man-made shade at Lee's Ferry. (Courtesy of the Dudley Humphrey Scott Collection; c. 1926.)

Albert "Bert" Loper was an explorer, miner, and river runner remembered best for his many colorful stories about his adventures along the Colorado. Here he stands in front of a billboard advertising river rides. (GRCA #5515; Courtesy of Dudley Humphrey Scott Collection.)

Nestled among the shadows at Lee's Ferry sat a service garage and store. Inside was a sign that advertised "Gas, Oil, Supplies, Iced Drinks And Never-Rip Overalls." (Courtesy of Dudley Humphrey Scott Collection.)

Coming from literally out of nowhere, desert sandstorms could prove devastating to man and machine alike. Here travelers try to find shelter as their automobiles are hit with a blast of sand. (Courtesy of the Dudley Humphrey Scott Collection.).

Attempts to traverse the many miles of the canyon demanded more than just ferry crossings. Here we see an early bridge designed to utilize suspension cables for support of a surface crossing as the Colorado makes its journey thousands of feet below. (Courtesy of the Dudley Humphrey Scott Collection.)

This side view of the Navajo Bridge construction shows the intricate detail of framework and girders. (GRCA #14645; c. 1927.)

This view, looking to the northeast of Navajo Bridge, shows construction nearing completion. Only the center section of the span remains to be set into place. (GRCA #14643; Courtesy of the Dudley Humphrey Scott Collection.)

Stringing cable high above the Colorado was surely not for the faint of heart. Because of their ability to work at dizzying heights, Indians were often hired to help with these projects. Adding to the construction difficulties was the often unrelenting desert heat. (GRCA #6258; c. 1927.)

Viewed from a distance downstream, the newly completed Navajo Bridge transports travelers safely over the Colorado. Note the gracefully arched design. (GRCA #14647; *c.* 1928.)

Children wearing hats and coveralls stand on one side of the Navajo Bridge. (GRCA #14598; *c.* 1927.)

The Scotts, along with other visitors to the area, enjoy a few minutes to stretch their legs and rest awhile by their automobiles. (Courtesy Dudley Humphrey Scott Collection.)

Louise Scott enjoys a ripe fig she has just picked from a tree. Vegetation is sparse due to the dry desert environment. (Courtesy of the Dudley Humphrey Scott Collection.)

A Congressional party takes a boat tour of the canyon's lower end. Note the dry, cracked mud in the foreground, stretching up to the side of the craft. (GRCA #9405; *c.* 1935.)

Here the Congressional party poses in front of the docks from which operators of separate boating companies compete for customers. The signs advertise Cashman's cruises (left) and the Emery Line (right). If you have exceptionally good eyesight, you can make out the cost of tickets on the Emery Line: adults 75¢; children 40¢. Who said the good old days weren't better? (GRCA #9411; *c.* 1935.)

Eight

TRAINS, PLANES, AND STAGECOACHES

A horse-drawn carriage prepares to depart from the El Tovar Hotel. At left, on the porch, a family sees them off. (GRCA #15523. Courtesy of the Fred Harvey Company; *c.* 1908.)

Travel by wagon was a slow and very dusty affair. Rough roads, lack of water, relentless heat, and dangerous river crossings were just some of the perils awaiting early travelers. (Courtesy of the Dudley Humphrey Scott Collection; *c.* 1920s.)

John Hance and William Hull were among the early developers of a stagecoach service from Flagstaff to the canyon. The trip was far from pleasant by today's standards. It was a hot, rough, two-day adventure over extremely primitive roads. Here, the Grandview Hotel Stage waits for passengers at the entrance of the El Tovar Hotel. (GRCA #12068; *c.* 1906.)

Theodore Roosevelt was succeeded in office as president by William Howard Taft in the election of 1908. Conservation was an important campaign issue, and coal miners and lumber companies actively opposed Roosevelt's stands and wanted to take government land reserves for themselves. Anti-conservationists were hopeful that with Roosevelt "retired" from political office, the public would return to earlier days of apathy. Here, the new president, not even one full year in office, visits the canyon—a visit which had many political overtones. (GRCA #5992A. Courtesy of the Fred Harvey Company; October 15, 1909.)

Despite the rugged journey to reach the canyon rim, the awesome vistas made the trip a memorable and worthwhile experience. (Courtesy of the Dudley Humphrey Scott Collection; *c. 1929.*)

In this view of the canyon, El Tovar can be seen in the distance. (Courtesy of the Dudley Humphrey Scott Collection; *c. 1929.*)

Truly a first of its kind, Oliver Lippincott is seen here arriving at the Grand Canyon's south rim driving the first steam-powered automobile. (GRCA #5122; January 12, 1902.)

Early visitors stand in front of the first passenger train carrying visitors from Williams to Grand Canyon, Arizona. The event sparked enough interest that newspapers all across the U.S. carried the story and awakened wide public interest, instigating what would later become a "boom" of visitors to the park. (GRCA #2435; September 17, 1901.)

Due in large measure to the railroad, passengers as well as provisions made their ways daily to the canyon. (Courtesy of the Dudley Humphrey Scott Collection.)

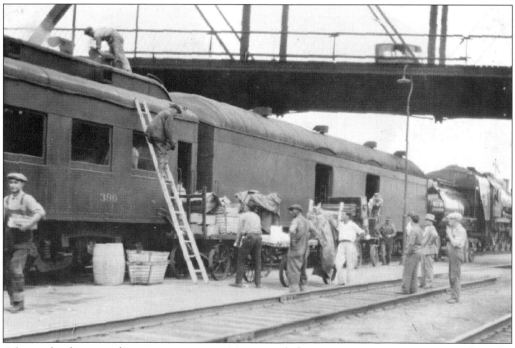

After unloading supplies, some canyon visitors used their own transportation to explore the Arizona desert. (Courtesy of the Dudley Humphrey Scott Collection.)

Shriner specials arrived at the Grand Canyon Station on March 28, 1937. Some Shriners are visible in this photo. This gathering was well attended, and members arrived on five different trains. (GRCA #859.)

More than half of the early visitors to the south rim of the canyon arrived by train at the Santa Fe Railway Station. This particular depot was built in 1909, in rustic design similar to many other facilities in the village. Verkamp's Curio Store can be seen at the upper right of the station. (GRCA #9465; *c.* 1940.)

Those choosing to travel by automobile needed a place to purchase fuel. Most had to rely on the Grand Canyon Service Station for both fuel and parts. (Courtesy of the Dudley Humphrey Scott Collection.)

A traveler checks his motorcycle as he prepares to use this distinct and unique mode of transportation to explore the canyon. (Courtesy of the Dudley Humphrey Scott Collection.)

Perhaps you can feel your own palms sweat as you contemplate the precarious position from which this visitor views the canyon. A close look at the right front wheel suggests our visitor took more protective care of his auto falling off the rim than he does of himself! (GRCA #16412.)

The DeHaviland airplane made the first recorded visit to the Grand Canyon and flew over its majestic expanse on February 25, 1919. (GRCA #5884.)

Standing next to a plane owned by Grand Canyon Airlines are, from left to right: Henry Langley, Irving Kravitz, and a ranger from Zion National Park. (GRCA #22; Summer 1931.)

At Old Red Butte, Grand Canyon Airport, park rangers, pilot, and passengers prepare to embark for a scenic view of the canyon rarely enjoyed by previous visitors. (GRCA #776; *c.* 1929.)

A row of Navy/Marine MB-2 bomber planes from San Diego visits Red Butte Field. (GRCA #65; June 14, 1932.)

Dudley Humphrey Scott personally designed and outfitted his car so as to transform it into a camping rig. A tent together with its frame can be seen extending to the left and rear of the vehicle. (GRCA #6824, Courtesy of the Dudley Humphrey Scott Collection; c. 1929.)

Following one of Scott's adventurous trips through the great Southwest, he was quoted as saying "Never saw a bridge over a culvert for over 400 miles. . . more water than usual." (Courtesy of the Dudley Humphrey Scott Collection; c. 1929.)

For the most part, road surfaces were difficult to travel, and comfort was almost non-existent by today's standards. Here the road runs up the bed of a stream (dry wash). (Courtesy of the Dudley Humphrey Scott Collection.)

Due to the designs of early automobiles, most of the luggage and provisions had to be strapped to the rear and on top of the roof. Dirt from the roadway was a constant irritant and source of discomfort. (Courtesy of the Dudley Humphrey Scott Collection.)

Dated August 1926, Dudley Humphrey Scott's car rests on a new road surface consisting mostly of loose gravel. From the looks of it, you still chose your "ruts" as much as you chose your "roads." (GRCA #6808; Courtesy of the Dudley Humphrey Scott Collection.)

Scott photographed this steam engine as it made its way into the canyon area with its cars of passengers. (Courtesy of the Dudley Humphrey Scott Collection.)

A more modern steam engine and cars, named the *School Train*, arrives at the Grand Canyon Yard in 1904. To the left, one can see the original depot (with workers on the porch) and boardwalk. (GRCA #5442.)

The Scotts made a fuel stop at the Eden Valley Filling Station. Their heavily loaded automobile is shown at right. (Courtesy of the Dudley Humphrey Scott Collection.)

Mary Jane Colter, shown here at age 33, designed many of the buildings on the canyon rim, taking great care to harmonize her designs with the natural environment. She modeled the Hopi House after part of the Hopi Village of Old Oraibi. Other designs to her credit were Phantom Ranch, the Watchtower, and Bright Angel Lodge. (GRCA #16950; *c.* 1892.)

Nine

THE CANYON'S SENTINEL

Standing proudly on the south rim of the canyon, the Fred Harvey Company's elegant El Tovar Hotel welcomes its visitors. Since its completion in 1905, the hotel remains a constant reminder of refinement, elegance, and splendor. This 1905 photo shows the dirt drive and "boardwalks" leading to the front entrance. It was often said that the hotel itself was worth a visit to the Grand Canyon. (GRCA #12088.)

The Fred Harvey Company attempted to revive an interest in Southwestern Indian arts and crafts. These Navajo Hogans, built in the shadow of the El Tovar Hotel, actually housed Navajo craftsmen. (GRCA #8123; July 1931.)

As with most park systems, growth in the area is controlled and very well planned. Here construction workers build a series of stairs and a walk leading to El Tovar.(GRCA #305; September 10, 1936.)

The front desk clerk and bellhop are ready for the first visitors in 1905. Designers of the hotel took great care to blend the building into the natural environment of the park outside. In this photo, note how the rustic appearance carries through to this area. The office and switchboard are also shown. Western Union provided telegraph service to the hotel lobby. (GRCA #9453.)

Seen here is a photo of a typical bedroom. Note the two sleigh beds—one double, one single. More than a hundred bedrooms were available with accommodations for 250 guests. (GRCA #9457.)

A breakfast room of El Tovar stands ready to welcome visitors to another adventurous day. Note the pictographic deer motif above the wood paneling. (GRCA #9451; *c.* 1905.)

The hotel featured the already famous "Harvey girls," dressed in black and white aprons and collars. Young women such as these set the standard for attentive and courteous service. (GRCA #6247D.)

Located above the office, the rotunda led to the mezzanine and ladies' lounging room. Charles Whittlesey, architect of El Tovar, used native stone and rustic pine logs from Oregon to produce this Swiss chalet motif. (GRCA #9452.)

Standing in front of the El Tovar Hotel, Mrs. Gargoza, secretary to the director of the National Park Service, is shown with her son (to her right). At her left is Ranger and naturalist Waesche and National Park Service Investigator Wilt. (GRCA #764.)

Arriving at the second floor, guests were cordially welcomed to a sunroom complete with roof gardens, majestic potted palms, and beautiful Persian rugs. This photo was taken on the occasion of the hotel's 1905 grand opening. (GRCA #9461.)

El Tovar was equipped with heat and electric lights powered by this steam generator located south of the hotel near the railroad tracks. (GRCA #9464; *c.* 1906.)

Silhouetted against the canyon's south rim, a picturesque view of El Tovar suggests why this hotel ranks among the most famous and splendid resort hotels in North America. The hotel was named after an officer in the army of Spanish explorer Coronado. (GRCA #48999.)

The billiard room, one of several amusement areas, was a favorite among guests who sought out the gaming tables for a bit of relaxation and entertainment at the end of a day. (GRCA #9456.)

Boasting accommodations said to be the finest in the West, travelers stepped from the rugged Arizona landscape into a luxury hotel, which featured first-class service fit for a king. (GRCA #9459.)

Many guests boarded buses or saw the sights from a Fred Harvey touring car. Well-trained driver/guides introduced guests to the beauties of the south rim. (GRCA #1390.)

The rendezvous room, with typical southwest design, features wood and stone so as to resemble a hunting lodge. Note the animal heads and guns. (GRCA #12085.)

The music room, another favorite spot to relax and reflect upon the day's events, offered guests a time to gather around the piano for a fun sing-along, or to simply pull a chair up to a table with some friends and reminisce. (GRCA #9460.)

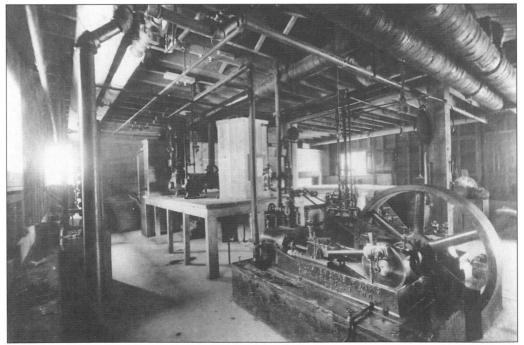

Railroads, once designed to transport rich deposits of ore, found new significance in transporting precious water. Once delivered, the water would be transferred to the hotel's filtering plant in the basement. In this photo we see the plant and hotel ice machine. (GRCA #9463.)

Evidence of many a stagecoach and horse-drawn wagon can be seen in these wheel impressions left behind in the dirt drive of El Tovar's entrance. (GRCA #9449.)

Simplistic and plain by today's standards perhaps, El Tovar's turn-of-the-century wine room and bar hosted many a weary traveler and would-be adventurer. One can only imagine the stories shared around this bar and across the tables. If only the walls could talk! A club room, barbershop, and art room were also available to guests. (GRCA #9458.)

Spectacular vistas along the south rim can take one's breath away. Around the trail, to the left, one can faintly see four figures seated on log benches taking in the sight near El Tovar. Mid-distance, a well-dressed gentleman with pipe in hand contemplates the view. (GRCA #18.)

Guests would be made comfortable in a bedroom suite, a corner of which is shown here. Note the lounge with pillows and an open book at center. A writing desk and wicker chair can be seen at right. Not seen, but ever present, were the spotless linens, costly silverware, and fine China crystal. (GRCA #9454.)

Pictured here are U.S. Senator Henry Fountain Ashurst, left, and El Tovar's manager, Vic Patrosso, right. On this occasion, the senator came to the park and spoke to an appreciative audience at the park's campground. It was through pioneering efforts such as his that legislation was eventually approved to create the Grand Canyon National Park and, at the same time, protect the rights of miners with valid land claims already established in the area. (GRCA #768.)

This is the kitchen of El Tovar. A true hallmark of hospitality and excellent cuisine, this impressive kitchen turned out many a memorable meal. Fresh fruits, vegetables, and flowers were grown in local greenhouses. Fresh eggs and milk were provided by the hotel's own farm animals. Trains from Santa Fe arrived daily bringing the best meat and freshest produce available. (GRCA #9450.)

With El Tovar Hotel watching from the edge of the south rim, a tourist takes advantage of a warm afternoon and poses for a picture. (GRCA #11414.)

Ten

CANYON WALLS AND VISTAS

D.H. Scott captured a view of travelers about to make their descent into the canyon. Trails such as this one wind their way down some 4,000 feet, making the return climb quite difficult. (Courtesy of the Dudley Humphrey Scott Collection.)

The first topographic map of the Grand Canyon was made by Francois Matthes, shown here with instrumentation. This plane table station and tethered umbrella were set up at Cape Royal. A second member of the crew records the necessary data. Matthes began the mapping two years earlier, in 1902, on the south rim. (GRCA #4453.)

An unnamed photographer captured an unforgettable picture of an anonymous woman pensively poised at the edge of a cliff 1 mile above the river . This 1905 photograph is thought-provoking, if not inspirational, in providing us a dimension of scale—how small we humans appear when compared with the greatness and wonder of nature. (GRCA #12001.)

Trail parties staying more than a day on Bright Angel or South Kaibab Trails would likely overnight at Phantom Ranch. The ranch got its name from Phantom Canyon, so named by the early surveyors who were struck by the illusory effect of the narrow gorge as seen from above in late afternoon. Others, however, say that Mary Colter, who designed the rustic cabins, named the ranch after a phantom in a Havasupai legend who supposedly emerged from an underworld tribe at this very spot on the canyon floor. (GRCA #13663.)

Dudley Humphrey Scott's touring car motors off into the desert bearing awesome testimony not only to the driver's adventurous spirit, but also his faith in a horseless carriage. One can only wonder what he would have done with one of today's four-by-four off-road explorers! (GRCA #6794; Courtesy of the Dudley Humphrey Scott Collection.)

Dudley Humphrey Scott takes a moment to ponder what life must have been like in these places generations ago. Mr. Scott was chief engineer at Euclid Beach Park in Cleveland, Ohio. Among other honors, he was president of the Cleveland Engineering Society for many years. His hobbies were his cameras and his travels to out-of-the-way corners of the desert Southwest with his wife, Louise. For many years he kept a car that he designed in the West, complete with camping equipment, to tour Yellowstone to the Colorado River. (GCNP Museum. Dudley Scott Collection; c. 1925.)

This view from Bright Angel Point on the north canyon rim looks southward. (GRCA #5000; *c.* 1900.)

Two horse-drawn coaches carry Grand Canyon visitors along the newly completed West Rim Drive. (GRCA #9605; December 5, 1911.)

This spectacular view is along the North Kaibab Trail, also known as "Hell's Kitchen." (GRCA #5542.)

This street scene of Walpi Village on Hopi First Mesa shows a narrow land bridge looking north. (GRCA #11329; *c.* 1918.)

This log dwelling is located in the woods near Rowe's well. Horses and wagons depicted a typical homestead. (GRCA #14710; *c.* 1898.)

Try as one might, it is difficult for the lens of a camera to transmit the breadth and depth of a scenic view such as this when one originally views it through the human eye. This photo, however, is one of Dudley Humphrey Scott's attempts at doing so. (Courtesy of the Dudley Humphrey Scott Collection.)

Here one gets some appreciation of scale! With the high canyon walls as background and the expansive desert brush in the foreground, look closely at the center right just ahead of the advancing late afternoon shadows, and you will see Goulding's Trading Post, Monument Valley, as it appeared in August of 1926. (GRCA #6796; Courtesy of the Dudley Humphrey Scott Collection.)

Striking a meditative silhouette, a lone Indian, wrapped in a blanket, looks down on Tonto Plateau from Hopi Point. (GRCA #12410; glass plate negative, *c.* 1900.)

Dated September 1899, this expansive view looks toward Apache Point from Mystic Springs Plateau. (GRCA #814. Glass plate negative, taken by Henry G. Peabody.)

This glass plate photo by Henry J. Peabody is entitled "On the Zig Zags of Bright Angel Trail." This 1902 photo was taken near Two Mile Corner and clearly shows the hazardous rocky terrain. Just one misstep by either horse or burro could spell painful injury or death. The best way to study this picture is to trace, with your finger, from the bottom center up the S-shaped trail to the upper left where a horse with rider appears to be straddling the trail. (GRCA #818.)

Pictured here is the Yavapai Observation Station (right, mid-distance) on the canyon's south rim. Notice how the structure, with its rock tower supports and plateau-shaped roof, blend so naturally and fittingly into the landscape. (GRCA #791.)

This scenic view of the high canyon walls stretches out beyond a tree-lined mountain in the foreground. (Courtesy of the Dudley Humphrey Scott Collection.)

Images such as this give one a feeling of the surreal, not unlike that of visiting a distant moon or planet. This particular view is taken from an old glass plate showing the lower section of Hermit Trail. (GRCA #12407.)

This stagecoach stops for a minute on the rim of the Grand Canyon. J.W. Thurber and passengers take in the view. (GRCA #4886.)

Eleven

TOURISM ON THE RIM

All of the hotels and restaurants along the Sante Fe railroad lines, including the dining cars, were operated by the Fred Harvey Company. Here, a Fred Harvey touring car motors up West Rim Drive with its cargo of tourists. El Tovar can be seen off in the distance. (GRCA #5426. Courtesy of the Fred Harvey Company; c. 1920.)

In what appears at first glance to be simply a large tent, is in fact a curio store. John George Verkamp, standing proudly in front of his place of business (here on the grounds of the Bright Angel Camp), would sell various Indian crafts and curios to tourists who wanted a souvenir or two to take home with them. Setting up shop was, for George, a fairly simple task and, like today's flea markets, he could move from one area to another with little waste of time and energy. (GRCA #5254.)

As the numbers of visitors increasingly grew from year to year, additional safety precautions had to be taken to protect the curious. In this 1935 photo, construction workers labor beneath a September sun to erect a rock wall guardrail in front of the El Tovar Hotel. (GRCA #329.)

Stephen T. Mather served as the first director of the National Park Service from 1916 to 1929. In this October 12, 1930 photo, naturalists Polly Patrow and Edwin McKee (front, kneeling) look on as staff members plant trees in Mather's memory. (GRCA #5765.)

The Civilian Conservation Corp (CCC) saw, as one of its most important goals, the continued preservation of the park's precious woodlands and forests. Pictured here are a group of enrollees transplanting healthy young pine trees. (GRCA #1409.)

Making its way along the canyon trail, a tourist car attempts the challenge of a tough climb up from the river. While appearing far different than its current off-road counterparts, these cars proved quite efficient and well up to the task. (GRCA #6765, Courtesy of the Dudley Scott Collection; mid-1920s.)

Should a visitor miss a tour bus, there was a second option—he or she could become part of what was called an auto caravan. Here, a line of some seven or eight cars, operated by their owners, travel single file to various tourist sites where, upon arrival, everyone would get out and join a park naturalist who would provide them with a short presentation of what they were about to view. Then, back into their cars they would go, and travel on to the next site on the tour. Striding to the rear of the first car, Park Naturalist Ralph Redburn prepares to start this caravan at the south rim. (GRCA #9389.)

Astride his horse and leading a party of three, John Hance (at left) starts down the Bright Angel Trail. (GRCA #823; photo taken by Henry G. Peabody, June 1902.)

What more spectacular and inspirational setting for an Easter sunrise service than this 1935 observance at the west rim worship site. Note the choir already in place to the left of the celebrants, standing at center in front of the large cross and altar. (GRCA #608.)

At Hopi Point, members of the Fifth Armored Division gather together to capture this inspirational view. Dated November 7, 1942, they were but one month away from the horrific anniversary of the bombing of Pearl Harbor. (GRCA #868.)

Pictured in June 1931, Pauline Mead Patraw, the first woman naturalist at the Grand Canyon, addresses members of an auto caravan on the East Rim Drive. (GRCA #173.)

Taking a welcome moment of reflective relaxation, a young woman in "flapper" dress appreciates the shade of a small pine tree as well as the majestic view at Yavapai Point looking toward Bright Angel Creek. (GRCA #12434; June 25, 1929.)

The desert of the great Southwest provides a marvelous habitat for a wide variety of animals that have successfully adapted to such an arid environment. Visitors are often treated to a spontaneous glimpse of a rock squirrel, mule deer, or gray fox hunting food or freely making their own tracks among the trails and ledges. Here Mrs. Scott enjoys feeding a very hungry fawn. (Courtesy of Dudley Humphrey Scott Collection.)

Tourists visit an Indian Trading Post. This one featured exquisitely woven Navajo rugs. (Courtesy of the Dudley Humphrey Scott Collection.)

Nestled around a small clump of shade trees, a tourist camp awaits its newest group of arrivals. Situated some 3,100 feet below the Canyon rim at Indian Gardens, this camp would be almost halfway down to the river. (GRCA #12065.)

The Grand View Hotel, seen here in the background, was said to be the best hotel on the rim from 1897, until El Tovar was opened in 1905. Pete Berry, seen here at right, was manager of the Grand View for many years. In this 1902 photo taken by Henry C. Peabody, Berry is about to lead this party of four down one of the canyon trails. (GRCA #826.)

Superintendent M.R. Tillotson shakes hands and greets two Hopi men in full headdress on their way to participate in park festivities in May of 1932. (GRCA #43.)

An unidentified park ranger stands on the porch of the old South Park Entrance station. Located on Highway 64 where several service roads came together, it stood some 300 yards south of the park's administration building. (GRCA #4.)

A close-up view of a Navajo hogan or house is shown above. Note the impressive rock walls and mud-covered roof with wood frame door. Navajo crafts were sold to visitors at the park's gift stores. (GRCA #6771; Courtesy of the Dudley Scott Collection.)

With the expansive canyon offering a scenic backdrop, Native American dancers perform for tourists at the Hopi House. (GRCA #15113.)

Built by the Harvey Company, Hopi House was designed for Hopi craftsmen as both a place to live and to display their many crafts. This ground-level room was the main sales area where tourists could purchase many a souvenir. (GRCA #11426.)

Native singers and dancers perform at the kiva dedication at Desert View Point. Note the tourists gathered on the steps in the upper left. The kiva is a copy of Indian ceremonial chambers where chieftains and elders of each tribe gathered for religious services and powwows. The watchtower structure duplicates that of early Indian towers. (GRCA #5419. Courtesy of the Fred Harvey Company; May 13, 1933.)

A Hopi clerk stands alongside a counter displaying a variety of crafts and souvenirs at the Desert View Watchtower shop. (GRCA #8502A; Courtesy of the Fred Harvey Company.)

This is the interior lobby of the Grand View Hotel. Spread beneath a rustic, low-slung ceiling, one can view a variety of rugs, displays, chairs, and a writing desk. At the far end of the room, note the hearth from which glowed many a welcoming fire. (GRCA #12090; c. 1900.)

Dated 1895, this photo shows a party of guests about to leave the Grand View Hotel and ride down the canyon trail on their burros. (GRCA #6254.)

Hotel accommodations on the north rim included the Grand Canyon Lodge. Seen here is a view of the expansive and elegant interior of the main dining room. (GRCA #13652; c. 1929.)

National Park Service staff Preston Patraw and his wife Polly spent their first ten years of marriage in this "Honeymoon Bungalow." (GRCA #6572; c. 1930.)

Major John Wesley Powell was the first to explore the Grand Canyon. He conducted two expeditions down the Colorado River, the first in 1869, and another in 1871. In his honor, this monument was erected on Powell Point and dedicated May 20, 1918. Approximately one year later, Frank Pinckley captured on film these two visitors carefully making their way up the monument stairs following a recent snowfall. A third visitor can be seen in the top left gazing contemplatively toward the western horizon. (GRCA #7281.)

"Do nothing to mar its grandeur. . . keep it for your children, your children's children, and all who come after you, as the one great sight which every American should see." (Theodore Roosevelt.)

In 1908, President Theodore Roosevelt established the Grand Canyon National Monument and placed the area under the jurisdiction of the United States Forest Service. A bill declaring the Grand Canyon a national park passed both houses of Congress and was signed by President Woodrow Wilson on February 26, 1919.

Seen here in a photo dated 1898, Theodore "Teddy" Roosevelt stands in front of his tent in full uniform as Colonel of the Rough Riders. (GRCA #7083.)